Adult Color By Numbers Coloring Book of

Mermaids

ZenMaster Coloring Books

COLOR TEST PAGE

COLOR TEST PAGE

1. Blue
2. Yellow
3. Red
4. Green
5. Dark Brown
6. Violet
7. Black
8. Light Blue
9. Light Yellow
10. Magenta
11. Forest Green
12. Brown
13. Tan
14. Dark Grey
15. Cyan
16. Orange
17. Light Magenta
18. Teal
19. Light Brown
20. Purple
21. Grey
22. Navy
23. Light Orange
24. Dark Red
25. Dark Green
26. Pink
27. Emerald Green

1. Blue
2. Yellow
3. Red
4. Green
5. Dark Brown
6. Violet
7. Black
8. Light Blue
9. Light Yellow
10. Magenta
11. Forest Green
12. Brown
13. Tan
14. Dark Grey
15. Cyan
16. Orange
17. Light Magenta
18. Teal
19. Light Brown
20. Purple
21. Grey
22. Navy
23. Light Orange
24. Dark Red
25. Dark Green
26. Pink
27. Emerald Green

1. Blue
2. Yellow
3. Red
4. Green
5. Dark Brown
6. Violet
7. Black
8. Light Blue
9. Light Yellow
10. Magenta
11. Forest Green
12. Brown
13. Tan
14. Dark Grey
15. Cyan
16. Orange
17. Light Magenta
18. Teal
19. Light Brown
20. Purple
21. Grey
22. Navy
23. Light Orange
24. Dark Red
25. Dark Green
26. Pink
27. Emerald Green

1. Blue
2. Yellow
3. Red
4. Green
5. Dark Brown
6. Violet
7. Black
8. Light Blue
9. Light Yellow
10. Magenta
11. Forest Green
12. Brown
13. Tan
14. Dark Grey
15. Cyan
16. Orange
17. Light Magenta
18. Teal
19. Light Brown
20. Purple
21. Grey
22. Navy
23. Light Orange
24. Dark Red
25. Dark Green
26. Pink
27. Emerald Green

1. Blue
2. Yellow
3. Red
4. Green
5. Dark Brown
6. Violet
7. Black
8. Light Blue
9. Light Yellow
10. Magenta
11. Forest Green
12. Brown
13. Tan
14. Dark Grey
15. Cyan
16. Orange
17. Light Magenta
18. Teal
19. Light Brown
20. Purple
21. Grey
22. Navy
23. Light Orange
24. Dark Red
25. Dark Green
26. Pink
27. Emerald Green

1. Blue
2. Yellow
3. Red
4. Green
5. Dark Brown
6. Violet
7. Black
8. Light Blue
9. Light Yellow
10. Magenta
11. Forest Green
12. Brown
13. Tan
14. Dark Grey
15. Cyan
16. Orange
17. Light Magenta
18. Teal
19. Light Brown
20. Purple
21. Grey
22. Navy
23. Light Orange
24. Dark Red
25. Dark Green
26. Pink
27. Emerald Green

1.   Blue
2.   Yellow
3.   Red
4.   Green
5.   Dark Brown
6.   Violet
7.   Black
8.   Light Blue
9.   Light Yellow
10. Magenta
11. Forest Green
12. Brown
13. Tan
14. Dark Grey
15. Cyan
16. Orange
17. Light Magenta
18. Teal
19. Light Brown
20. Purple
21. Grey
22. Navy
23. Light Orange
24. Dark Red
25. Dark Green
26. Pink
27. Emerald Green

1. Blue
2. Yellow
3. Red
4. Green
5. Dark Brown
6. Violet
7. Black
8. Light Blue
9. Light Yellow
10. Magenta
11. Forest Green
12. Brown
13. Tan
14. Dark Grey
15. Cyan
16. Orange
17. Light Magenta
18. Teal
19. Light Brown
20. Purple
21. Grey
22. Navy
23. Light Orange
24. Dark Red
25. Dark Green
26. Pink
27. Emerald Green

1. Blue
2. Yellow
3. Red
4. Green
5. Dark Brown
6. Violet
7. Black
8. Light Blue
9. Light Yellow
10. Magenta
11. Forest Green
12. Brown
13. Tan
14. Dark Grey
15. Cyan
16. Orange
17. Light Magenta
18. Teal
19. Light Brown
20. Purple
21. Grey
22. Navy
23. Light Orange
24. Dark Red
25. Dark Green
26. Pink
27. Emerald Green

1. Blue
2. Yellow
3. Red
4. Green
5. Dark Brown
6. Violet
7. Black
8. Light Blue
9. Light Yellow
10. Magenta
11. Forest Green
12. Brown
13. Tan
14. Dark Grey
15. Cyan
16. Orange
17. Light Magenta
18. Teal
19. Light Brown
20. Purple
21. Grey
22. Navy
23. Light Orange
24. Dark Red
25. Dark Green
26. Pink
27. Emerald Green

1. Blue
2. Yellow
3. Red
4. Green
5. Dark Brown
6. Violet
7. Black
8. Light Blue
9. Light Yellow
10. Magenta
11. Forest Green
12. Brown
13. Tan
14. Dark Grey
15. Cyan
16. Orange
17. Light Magenta
18. Teal
19. Light Brown
20. Purple
21. Grey
22. Navy
23. Light Orange
24. Dark Red
25. Dark Green
26. Pink
27. Emerald Green

1. Blue
2. Yellow
3. Red
4. Green
5. Dark Brown
6. Violet
7. Black
8. Light Blue
9. Light Yellow
10. Magenta
11. Forest Green
12. Brown
13. Tan
14. Dark Grey
15. Cyan
16. Orange
17. Light Magenta
18. Teal
19. Light Brown
20. Purple
21. Grey
22. Navy
23. Light Orange
24. Dark Red
25. Dark Green
26. Pink
27. Emerald Green

1. Blue
2. Yellow
3. Red
4. Green
5. Dark Brown
6. Violet
7. Black
8. Light Blue
9. Light Yellow
10. Magenta
11. Forest Green
12. Brown
13. Tan
14. Dark Grey
15. Cyan
16. Orange
17. Light Magenta
18. Teal
19. Light Brown
20. Purple
21. Grey
22. Navy
23. Light Orange
24. Dark Red
25. Dark Green
26. Pink
27. Emerald Green

1. Blue
2. Yellow
3. Red
4. Green
5. Dark Brown
6. Violet
7. Black
8. Light Blue
9. Light Yellow
10. Magenta
11. Forest Green
12. Brown
13. Tan
14. Dark Grey
15. Cyan
16. Orange
17. Light Magenta
18. Teal
19. Light Brown
20. Purple
21. Grey
22. Navy
23. Light Orange
24. Dark Red
25. Dark Green
26. Pink
27. Emerald Green

1. Blue
2. Yellow
3. Red
4. Green
5. Dark Brown
6. Violet
7. Black
8. Light Blue
9. Light Yellow
10. Magenta
11. Forest Green
12. Brown
13. Tan
14. Dark Grey
15. Cyan
16. Orange
17. Light Magenta
18. Teal
19. Light Brown
20. Purple
21. Grey
22. Navy
23. Light Orange
24. Dark Red
25. Dark Green
26. Pink
27. Emerald Green

1. Blue
2. Yellow
3. Red
4. Green
5. Dark Brown
6. Violet
7. Black
8. Light Blue
9. Light Yellow
10. Magenta
11. Forest Green
12. Brown
13. Tan
14. Dark Grey
15. Cyan
16. Orange
17. Light Magenta
18. Teal
19. Light Brown
20. Purple
21. Grey
22. Navy
23. Light Orange
24. Dark Red
25. Dark Green
26. Pink
27. Emerald Green

1. Blue
2. Yellow
3. Red
4. Green
5. Dark Brown
6. Violet
7. Black
8. Light Blue
9. Light Yellow
10. Magenta
11. Forest Green
12. Brown
13. Tan
14. Dark Grey
15. Cyan
16. Orange
17. Light Magenta
18. Teal
19. Light Brown
20. Purple
21. Grey
22. Navy
23. Light Orange
24. Dark Red
25. Dark Green
26. Pink
27. Emerald Green

1. Blue
2. Yellow
3. Red
4. Green
5. Dark Brown
6. Violet
7. Black
8. Light Blue
9. Light Yellow
10. Magenta
11. Forest Green
12. Brown
13. Tan
14. Dark Grey
15. Cyan
16. Orange
17. Light Magenta
18. Teal
19. Light Brown
20. Purple
21. Grey
22. Navy
23. Light Orange
24. Dark Red
25. Dark Green
26. Pink
27. Emerald Green

1. Blue
2. Yellow
3. Red
4. Green
5. Dark Brown
6. Violet
7. Black
8. Light Blue
9. Light Yellow
10. Magenta
11. Forest Green
12. Brown
13. Tan
14. Dark Grey
15. Cyan
16. Orange
17. Light Magenta
18. Teal
19. Light Brown
20. Purple
21. Grey
22. Navy
23. Light Orange
24. Dark Red
25. Dark Green
26. Pink
27. Emerald Green

1. Blue
2. Yellow
3. Red
4. Green
5. Dark Brown
6. Violet
7. Black
8. Light Blue
9. Light Yellow
10. Magenta
11. Forest Green
12. Brown
13. Tan
14. Dark Grey
15. Cyan
16. Orange
17. Light Magenta
18. Teal
19. Light Brown
20. Purple
21. Grey
22. Navy
23. Light Orange
24. Dark Red
25. Dark Green
26. Pink
27. Emerald Green

Thank you for supporting
ZenMaster Coloring Books

Your support means the world to us,
and we're thrilled to have you embark on this
creative journey with us.

Our small company strives to make a
BIG difference by helping those
who may be less fortunate.

This is why we proudly hire struggling
artists from around the world!

Our goal is to provide financial support to artists and
their families by enabling them to pursue their passions
and share their hard work and limitless talent with you!

Help support our hard working artists
by leaving a positive review on Amazon!

And follow us on Facebook for updates and
FREE COLORING PAGES!
https://www.facebook.com/zenmastercoloringbooks/

Check out more of our books at:
amazon.com/author/zenmastercoloringbooks

Free Bonus Page!
from:

Extreme dot to dot book of
Butterflies and Flowers

https://amzn.com/dp/1717596746

Also available in color by numbers!!
https://www.amazon.com/dp/1977932398

And a non-numbered edition
https://www.amazon.com/dp/1977882978

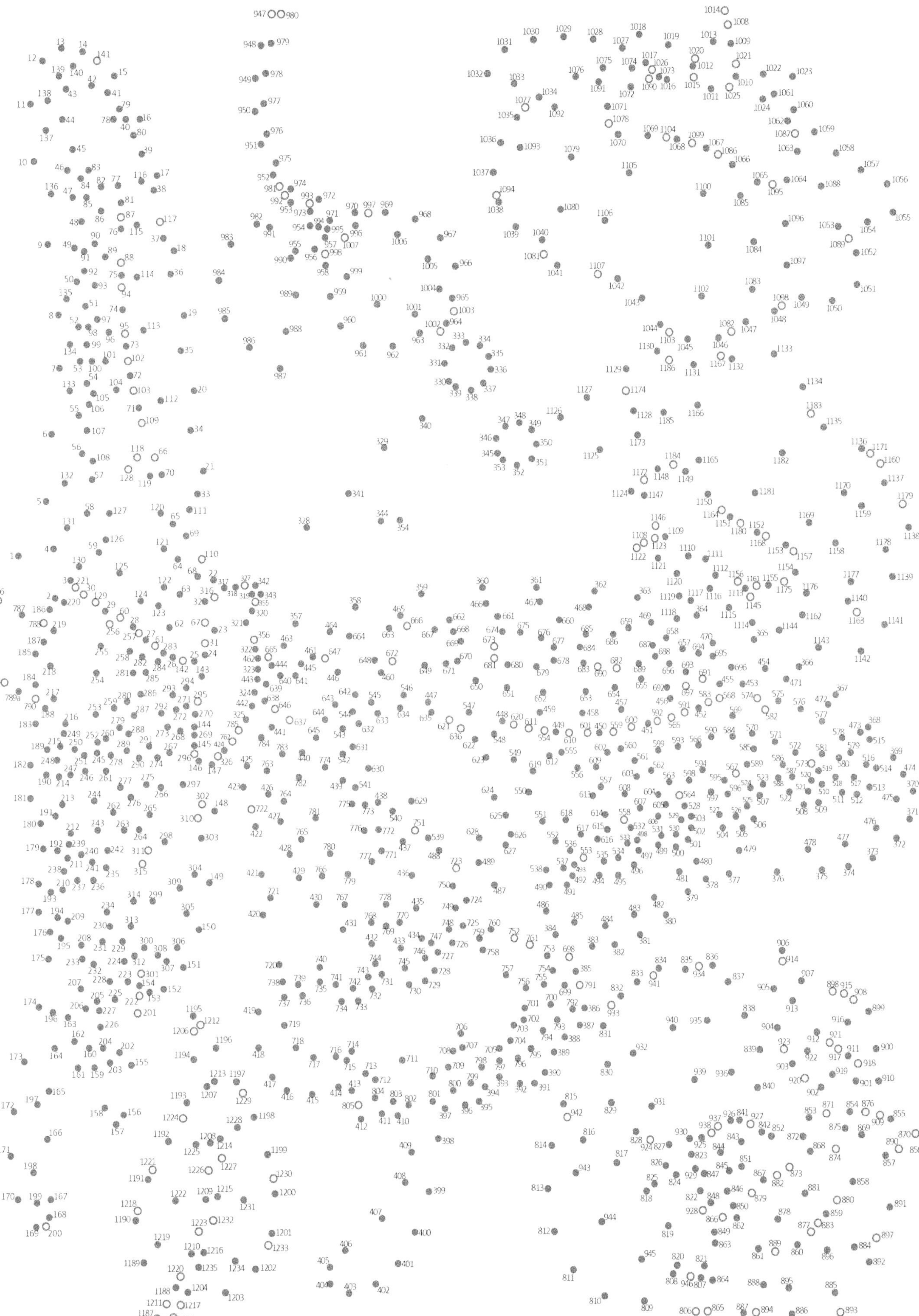

Free Bonus Page!
from:

Adult Coloring Book of
Island Dreams Vacation

https://www.amazon.com/dp/1976291267

Also available in color by numbers!!

https://www.amazon.com/dp/1976507707

And 5x8" Travel Size

https://www.amazon.com/dp/1796516090

Free Bonus Page!
from:

Kittens and Cats
coloring book for adults

https://www.amazon.com/dp/1977939619

Also available in color by numbers!!

https://www.amazon.com/dp/1979069018

And 5x8" Travel Size

https://www.amazon.com/dp/1727552628

Free Bonus Page!
from:

Koi Fish
coloring book for adults

https://www.amazon.com/dp/1977939619

Also available in color by numbers!!
https://www.amazon.com/dp/198149104x

And 5x8" Travel Size
https://www.amazon.com/dp/1727375149

Free Bonus Page!
from:

Adult Coloring Book of
Chihuahuas

https://www.amazon.com/dp/1796764191

Also available in color by numbers!!

https://www.amazon.com/dp/1977932398

And a 5x8" Travel Size

https://www.amazon.com/dp/1797722158

Free Bonus Page!
from:

Zen Coloring Notebook

https://www.amazon.com/dp/1535457015

Available in 9 different colors!

Also available in 5x8" journal size

https://www.amazon.com/dp/1535540591